SCHOLASTIC

Hands-On History

Civil War

by Michael Gravois

New York • Toronto • London • Auckland • Sydney *Teaching*
Mexico City • New Delhi • Hong Kong • Buenos Aires *Resources*

Dedication

To my brother, Keith Gravois—
compatriot, Southerner, and friend

Keith and Angie Gravois with their sons, Logan and Kyle

Cover design by Jason Robinson
Interior design by Michael Gravois
Interior illustrations by Jim Palmer and Mona Mark

ISBN 0-439-41125-4

2 3 4 5 6 7 8 9 10   40   11 10 09 08 07 06 05

Table of Contents

Introduction

As a middle-school teacher, I was always looking for ways to keep students interested and enthusiastic about learning. I developed activities and projects that helped me teach the required curriculum and also made my lessons fun, hands-on, diverse, and challenging.

I used an interactive-project approach with my fifth-grade students, and I can't stress enough how much they enjoyed it. Throughout each unit I had my students keep the activity sheets and projects in a pocket folder, so they could assemble a student-made textbook on the subject we were studying. They used these textbooks as a study guide for the final test. I was amazed at the higher-level thinking that took place in class discussions and by the degree of knowledge students had acquired by the end of each unit. Parents even commented on the unique way the information was presented and how easy it was for their children to study for the final test. After seeing my students' success, I decided to put my ideas on paper. *Hands-On History: The Civil War* is a compilation of the activities I used to teach the Civil War.

For each activity and project, I've included detailed instructions. Many of the activities incorporate language arts and critical thinking skills, such as differentiating fact and opinion, comparing and contrasting, the 5 Ws (who, what, where, when, why), understanding cause and effect, writing a letter, brainstorming, and sequencing.

I hope your students enjoy these projects as much as mine did.

How to Use This Book

Supplies

At the beginning of the school year, ask students to bring in the materials needed to create the projects throughout the year. Also arrange the classroom desks into clusters, each with a bin to hold pens, markers, glue sticks, scissors, and other needed supplies. This enables students to share the materials. You should have each of your students bring in the following supplies:

- a roll of tape
- several glue sticks
- a good pair of scissors
- a packet of colored pencils
- a packet of thin, colored markers
- a project folder (pocket type) to hold papers and other project materials

Maximizing Learning

Because different students have different learning styles, you may first want to orally summarize the information you will be covering that day. Then you can read the related section in a textbook or trade book. Finally, have students complete the activity. This not only exposes visual, aural, and artistic learners to the information through their strongest learning style, but it also allows all students to review the same information several times.

Civil War Vocabulary Bulletin Board

Materials: copies of page 27, colored bulletin board paper, craft sticks

At the beginning of your Civil War unit, set up a vocabulary bulletin board that students add to as the unit unfolds. First, cover the bulletin board with blue paper for the sky, white paper for clouds, and green paper for grass. Then line the horizon with a split-rail fence made out of craft sticks. Across the top add a title banner that reads "Civil War Vocabulary."

Students take turns writing each new vocabulary word and its definition on the "vocabulary blast" cutouts from the reproducible on page 27. They may color the blast if they wish. Keep a supply of "vocabulary blasts" handy for students to use as new words come up in class. See the list below for some suggestions.

Word List

abolitionist: a person who worked to end slavery in the United States

amendment: a change in the law, especially a change in the U.S. Constitution

baggage: slaves who traveled on the Underground Railroad

black codes: laws passed by Southern states after the Civil War that limited the rights of newly freed African Americans

border states: slaveholding states that remained loyal to the Union

bunker: a mound of dirt or a trench used by soldiers for protection from gunfire

carpetbagger: the name given to Northerners who moved to the South after the Civil War

civil war: a war in which people from the same country fight against each other

conductor: a person who guided slaves to freedom along the Underground Railroad

emancipate: to free

Rebel: a Northern nickname for a Confederate soldier

secede: to leave a group, such as when the Confederate states left the Union

segregation: the separation of people, often by race

sharecroppers: poor farmers who rented land from a landowner and paid rent with crops they grew there

spiritual: a religious folk song that originated among African-American slaves

station: a safe place where escaped slaves could stay along the Underground Railroad

stationmaster: a person who ran a station along the Underground Railroad

Yankee: a Southern nickname for a Union soldier

Home/School Communication

Before beginning a new unit with your class, send a letter home to students' families informing them of what you will be studying. Also ask the families for help if they have special knowledge or experience relating to the subject you are studying. At right is a sample letter.

Dear _____

For the next few weeks, our social studies curriculum will focus on the Civil War period. We will study the events that led up the war, inventions of the time, costumes and uniforms, famous figures, significant battles, and the effects of prejudice. While we study this subject, your child will be introduced to quality literature that reflects life during this troubled time in American history.

If you have any family histories that date back to the Civil War, please share them with your child so he or she can tell them to the class. Or better yet, feel free to come to our class to share your stories directly.

As usual, I ask that if you have any novels, photography books, memorabilia, or other items related to the Civil War theme, please consider allowing your child to bring them to class. Please make sure your name is on any items brought to class.

Thank you for your help. If you have any questions or suggestions, or if you would like to make an appointment to visit our class, you can reach me at [telephone number].

Sincerely,

Freedom Quilts: The Underground Railroad

Materials: copies of page 28, scissors, rulers, colored markers, tape

Reference Books: *Sweet Clara and the Freedom Quilt* by Deborah Hopkinson (Random House, 1995), *Aunt Harriet's Underground Railroad in the Sky* by Faith Ringgold (Crown, 1995)

Before the Civil War began, many slaves sought freedom by traveling along the Underground Railroad from Southern states to the North. A good way to introduce students to this subject is to read about it with the class and share picture books related to the topic, such as my favorites listed above.

The story of Underground Railroad quilts is a mixture of fact and fiction. Since it was illegal in most states for slaves to learn to read and write, some historians believe that images on quilts were used to provide slaves with clues about safe paths to freedom. Other historians say that there is no evidence that this actually occurred. However, these stories have filled our imaginations with visions of quilts as part of the flight for freedom.

CREATING THE QUILT BLOCK

1. Read aloud *Sweet Clara and the Freedom Quilt* and *Aunt Harriet's Underground Railroad in the Sky*. Discuss the theory that quilts may have served to guide people escaping slavery.

2. Give students copies of the quilt template and have them use geometric shapes and patterns to illustrate a hidden message about the Underground Railroad. Have students color the shapes so that they look like pieces of fabric and then cut out their quilt blocks. On the back of their freedom quilt blocks, ask them to write a paragraph describing the message that their blocks convey. Encourage students to be creative with the messages they'd like to illustrate. Some suggestions are at right.

3. Have each student explain the meaning of his or her quilt block to the class. Then hang the blocks next to each other in a grid to form a class freedom quilt.

Suggested Quilt Messages

- This house is a safe station.
- Follow the North Star to freedom.
- Take a zigzag route to avoid slave hunters.
- Travel after the sun goes down.
- Wade across streams to hide your scent from dogs.
- You can find food and water here.
- Do not stop in this town; it is not safe.
- Slave hunters are in this area.
- Follow the bank along the west side of the lake.

Road Map to the Civil War

Materials: 12" by 18" white construction paper or poster board, colored markers or pencils

For this project, students create time lines using the format of a road map. Their "road maps" will highlight important events in the United States that led up to the Civil War.

CREATING THE ROAD MAP

1. Have students read the lessons in their textbooks about life before the Civil War and keep a list of ten important events, laws, and actions that led up to the war.

2. Provide white construction paper or poster board. Have students design a road that has a beginning and end. It can be a winding country road, a busy main street, a superhighway, or a design of their choice. Advise students to use pencil when designing the road in case they need to make changes.

CONTINUED ON PAGE 8

CREATING THE ROAD MAP (*CONTINUED*)

3. Have students design a "stop" along the road for each event on their list. The stops can be traffic lights, stop signs, yield signs, bridges, exit ramps, detours, toll booths, road hazards, buildings, and so on. Make sure that they label each stop with the name and date of the event. The events should be added to the road map in sequential order, starting at the beginning of the road and ending with the title "The Civil War."

4. Ask students to write two complete sentences under the title of each stop that describe important and interesting information about the event.

Suggested Stops

- Slavery
- Missouri Compromise
- Fugitive Slave Law
- Compromise of 1850
- *Uncle Tom's Cabin*
- Kansas-Nebraska Act
- Dred Scott Decision
- John Brown's Raid
- Lincoln's Election
- Confederate States of America
- Attack on Fort Sumter

5. After students have designed their road maps and their stops, have them fill up empty space by illustrating details related to each event, such as the problem or issue, the place, and the people involved. (You might have students design their road maps first with a predetermined number of stops. Then they can add information and visual details to the road maps as you read about new topics in the textbook.)

6. Next, have students fold the road maps as shown below and use creative lettering to write a map title on the small square panel at the front.

7. Finally, have students lift the title panels to reveal a blank long vertical panel. On this panel, ask students to write two complete paragraphs describing the United States in the years leading up to the Civil War.

1. Fold the map in half so that the illustration is on the outside.

2. Fold the top and bottom panels back toward the first fold.

3. Fold the top half of the map down.

Letters to President Lincoln: Three Points of View

Materials: envelopes, paper, colored markers or pencils

Integrate persuasive writing into your Civil War unit with a letter-writing campaign to President Lincoln.

CREATING THE LETTERS

1. Lead a discussion about the different points of view that were held by plantation owners, slaves, and abolitionists before the Civil War.

2. Divide the class into three groups, with each group focusing on one point of view.

3. Ask each student to write a letter to President Lincoln from the point of view of his or her group (regardless of whether the student agrees with that point of view), trying to convince Lincoln of the merits of this position.

4. Have students design stationery for the final version of their letters by creating a border related to the author's viewpoint (e.g., cotton bolls for the plantation owner). Have them address envelopes and design appropriate stamps. Divide a bulletin board into three sections and hang the letters and envelopes. Finally, create a banner that reads "Letters to President Lincoln: Three Points of View."

Abe Lincoln's Résumé: The Man for the Job

One good way to find out about a person's professional background and interests is to look at his or her résumé. In this activity, students create a professional profile fo the 16th U.S. president.

CREATING THE RÉSUMÉ

1. Have your students research the life of Abraham Lincoln, concentrating on his education, work experience, and interests.

2. Using this information, have them create a résumé for Lincoln reflecting his accomplishments at the time he ran for president in 1860. Show the class samples of résumés that use different layouts and features. You might even let them learn more about your own background and qualifications by showing them your résumé.

3. If you have computers in your classroom or a computer lab in your school, have students type the résumé and print it out so it looks even more professional.

The Clincher: Both Sides Expect to Win

Materials: copies of page 29, white copier paper

Leaders from both the North and South expected to win the Civil War. Each side had distinct advantages over the other. Help your students learn about the advantages and disadvantages of both sides by creating "clinchers," which they can use to quiz one another on this topic.

CREATING THE CLINCHER

1. Hand out a copy of page 29 and a sheet of copier paper to each student.

2. Review with students the directions on page 29 for how to create the clinchers. You may want to work as a class, following the steps as shown on the reproducible together.

3. After students have completed folding and numbering their clinchers, explain that they will use them to create a quiz about the strengths of the North and the South during the Civil War. Under each of the eight numbered inside panels, have students write one advantage of the North or the South. They should write four for each side, for a total of eight, and label the panels "North" or "South," according to the advantage listed.

4. Have students quiz one another using the clinchers. One student picks a number from 1 to 10 and the other opens and closes the clincher that many times. Then the first student picks a flap number and the second reads the advantage listed under the flap. The first student guesses whether the North or the South had this advantage. Encourage students to create variations on this quiz to learn about the advantages of the North and South.

Suggested Answers

ADVANTAGES FOR THE NORTH
- larger population
- more resources and factories to make supplies
- grew more food
- more railroads to move supplies and troops

ADVANTAGES FOR SOUTH
- better officers to lead the army
- soldiers grew up riding horses and using guns to hunt
- fighting a defensive war to preserve their way of life
- fighting on their own territory

NNNNNNNNNNNNNNNNNNNNNNNNNNNNNNNNNNN

Matchbook of a Nation Divided

Materials: copies of pages 30 and 31, scissors, colored markers

In this activity, students learn how the geography of the United States changed during the Civil War.

CREATING THE MATCHBOOK

1. First, copy the reproducibles on pages 30 and 31 so that the map and the title strip are on one side and the questions are *inverted* on the other, as shown at right.

2. Have students place the papers in front of them so that the questions are faceup. Have them fold up the title strips at the bottom and crease along the line. Then have them fold down the top half of their pages so that it tucks underneath the title strip.

3. Next, have students color the maps and keys to show the Union states, the Confederate states, and the border states (slave states that stayed in the Union).

4. Have students use the map to answer the questions in the matchbook.

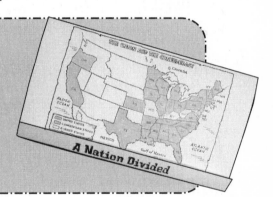

Answers for Matchbooks

1. Five: Missouri, Kentucky, West Virginia, Maryland, Delaware
2. Nineteen
3. Eleven
4. West Virginia split from Virginia
5. On the border between the Union and Confederacy, near the border states

Famous Men Jumping Jacks

Materials: copies of page 32, poster board, scissors, hole punch, colored markers, glue sticks, brass paper fasteners, string, awl or compass point, construction paper, assorted craft materials (for costume)

In this activity, students create jumping jacks of famous men from the Civil War era. Encourage students to choose a famous man from this period and research his life. A list of some names is provided on page 12. After students have completed their research, have them follow directions for creating a jumping jack, personalizing it with details that they have learned about that person's life.

11

CREATING THE JUMPING JACK

1. Provide students with copies of the reproducible on page 32. Have them cut out the pieces of the template and trace them onto poster board. Students should refer to the illustration on the reproducible while assembling their projects.

2. Have students use a pencil to mark the five points where small holes will be made. (An awl or compass point works well.) Then ask students to mark the 16 points for the large holes and use a hole punch to make these holes.

3. Have students lay the body parts in place faceup and decide what kind of clothing their figures would wear. Invite them to color clothing and a face on their jumping jacks. Suggest that they might even create hats, shoes, and other clothing to glue on, and add a special "prop" to their characters' hands.

4. Have students attach the arms and the legs to the body by pushing the brass fasteners through the eight large holes.

5. Instruct students to place their jumping jacks facedown and attach a short piece of string to the two shoulder holes, tying a double knot at both ends. Have them do the same with the hip holes. They should refer to the illustration on the reproducible for help.

6. Have students tie one end of a piece of string to the center of the shoulder string and connect it to the center of the hip string with another knot. Remind them to leave an extra length of string at the bottom, extending about 3" below the feet.

7. Finally, have students tie a 6" piece of string to the hole in the top of the head.

8. Show students how to hold the upper string with one hand and pull on the lower string with the other hand to animate their historical jumping jack.

Famous Men of the Civil War Era

P. G. T. Beauregard
John Wilkes Booth
Mathew Brady
John Brown
Ambrose E. Burnside
John C. Calhoun
Jefferson Davis
Stephen A. Douglas
Frederick Douglass
Ulysses S. Grant
Horace Greeley
Thomas "Stonewall" Jackson
Andrew Johnson
Robert E. Lee
Abraham Lincoln
George B. McClellan
George Meade
George Pickett
Hiram Revels
William H. Seward
William Tecumseh Sherman
Nat Turner
Walt Whitman

Famous Women People Books

Materials: white construction paper, scissors, assorted craft materials, colored markers or pencils

The Civil War was not fought by men alone. Women from both the North and South played important roles in the war effort. Many women took over men's jobs on farms when their husbands and fathers went off to fight. Some women even disguised themselves as men and fought bravely in battles throughout the war. Others worked tirelessly as nurses to care for the sick and wounded.

To help your class understand the contributions of some of these women, have students create "people books" of women from the Civil War. Have them follow the directions on page 14 to create the books. First, they should chose a woman and research her life and contributions to the Civil War. Below is a list of suggested subjects for this activity.

· HARRIET TUBMAN ·

Harriet Tubman was born on a Maryland plantation and worked as a field slave until she escaped in 1849. She was thirty years old. She continued to lead slaves from slavery on the Underground Railroad. She made her trips during the winter, when the nights were long and fewer people were outside their homes. During the day she and the fugitive slaves hide in barns and swamps, or in the homes of abolitionists. Sometimes she used disguises. In her eight years as a "conductor" she never lost a passenger. She is a true role model of bravery and generosity.

Famous Women of the Civil War Era

Clara Barton	Angelina and Sarah Grimké
Mary Ann Bickerdyke	Elizabeth Keckley
Malinda Blalock	Susie King
Mary Elizabeth Bowser	Mary Curtis Lee
Belle Boyd	Mary Todd Lincoln
Mary Chestnut	Harriet Beecher Stowe
Pauline Cushman	Mary Surratt
Varina Howell Davis	Sally Tompkins
Dorothea Dix	Sojourner Truth
Sarah Emma Edmonds	Harriet Tubman
Charlotte Forten	Loreta Velazquez
Rose Greenhow	Mary Edwards Walker

CREATING THE
FAMOUS WOMEN PEOPLE BOOKS

1. Ask students to fold a sheet of white construction paper in half twice horizontally and then once vertically.

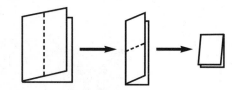

2. Have them open it up to reveal eight panels.

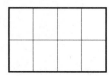

3. Instruct students to cut the bottom left and bottom right panels along the dotted lines, as shown. Have them save the two scraps of paper.

4. Next, have students fold in the top left and top right panels.

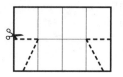

5. Then ask students to glue the two scraps that were cut away behind the top two panels, as shown.

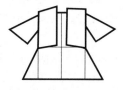

6. Have students add a head, legs, and hands to the figure.

7. Tell students to use buttons, markers, fabrics, dimensional glue, and other craft materials to decorate the figure. They can create clothing that is representative of the historical figure.

8. Using construction paper, students should create an object to put in the figure's hand that is relevant to her accomplishment.

9. Ask students to write—inside the two flaps—two complete, detailed paragraphs describing the significance and the accomplishments of the woman on whom they are reporting.

10. Finally, have students prepare an oral report on this woman to give to the class.

Circle Book of Famous Battles

Materials: copies of pages 33–35, scissors, glue sticks, colored markers or pencils

In this activity, students will choose an important battle from the Civil War and create a circle book that describes its significance.

CREATING THE CIRCLE BOOK

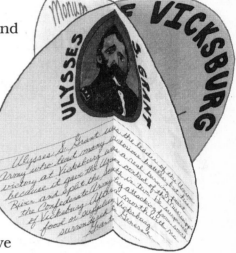

1. Provide students with one copy each of pages 33 and 34 and two copies each of page 35.

2. Let students choose an important battle from the Civil War. On the drawing template (page 1 of the circle books), have students write the name and date of the battle and draw a picture or a map of the battle.

3. On the writing template (page 2), have students write a brief account of the battle, describing who was involved, why and where it took place, and what the results were.

4. On the first drawing/writing template (page 3), have students report on a famous person associated with the battle. Have them draw a picture of the person at the top and write a description about the person in the bottom half of the circle.

5. On the second drawing/writing template (page 4), ask students to design a monument for their battlefield and draw it at the top of the page. Below their pictures, have them include a paragraph explaining the monuments' design and significance.

6. After they have completed their reports, have students cut out the four circles and fold each in half.

7. Instruct students to glue the right half of page 1 to the left half of page 2 as shown below. Then have them glue the right half of page 2 to the left half of page 3, and the left half of page 3 to the left half of page 4. Finally, ask them to complete the circle book by gluing the right half of page 4 to the left half of page 1.

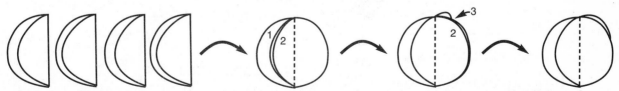

Display Idea: Hang a string high across your classroom. Tie varying lengths of thread from the string at intervals across the room. Tie a paper clip to the end of each piece of thread and hang a circle book from each paper clip. When a breeze blows, the circle books spin and create a vibrant display to jazz up the classroom.

The Age of Ironclad Ships

Materials: copies of page 36, aluminum foil, colored markers or pencils, glue sticks

The invention of steam power in the 1800s meant that heavier ships could be built. Both the Union and Confederate navies covered wooden ships with thick iron plates, which allowed them to better withstand the blasts of cannon fire. Have students work in pairs to research some of the ironclad ships from the Civil War. Then have them complete the activity.

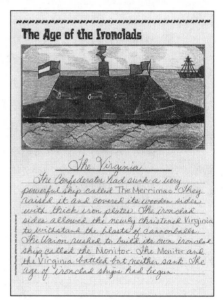

CREATING THE IRONCLAD SHIP REPORT

1. Provide students with copies of page 36.

2. Have students choose a ship from their research and draw a picture of it in the box. Then have them write the name of the ship on the center line and a paragraph describing it on the lines below.

3. Have students place a piece of aluminum foil underneath their picture and trace the outline of the hull with a sharp pencil, making an impression on the foil. Then ask them to cut out the foil panel and glue it to the ship.

4. Have student pairs present their reports to the class.

Emancipation Proclamation Elevator Book

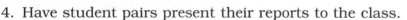

Materials: copies of page 37

After reading about the Emancipation Proclamation, distribute copies of the template on page 37. Explain to students that in this activity they will examine how the Emancipation Proclamation was perceived differently in the North and in the South.

CREATING THE ELEVATOR BOOK

1. Have students bend the left and right panels backward, creasing along the folds. The rectangular panel shows the illustration of the proclamation.

CONTINUED ON PAGE 17

16

CREATING THE ELEVATOR BOOK (CONTINUED)

2. Show students how to pull the left and right edges in toward the center of the rectangle so that the two edges meet. Have them press down and crease along the folds to create folded panels that open like elevator doors.

3. Ask students to open the "elevator doors" to reveal the center panel. In this area, have them write a complete description of the Emancipation Proclamation and its intended purpose.

4. On the side panels—under the elevator doors—have students list ways the proclamation was received and interpreted differently in the North and in the South, and the effect it had on each.

Suggested Answers

CENTER PANEL

President Lincoln issued the Emancipation Proclamation in 1862. It stated that as of January 1, 1863, all slaves in the Confederate states were free. This proclamation ended slavery in the South. However, slavery was still allowed in the slave states that had stayed in the Union.

NORTH

- Northern abolitionists were overjoyed.
- Some white Northerners were angry that Lincoln took this drastic step.
- The Union army could now recruit more black soldiers.
- European countries were more likely to support the North.
- The United States was now a free society.

SOUTH

- Most white Southerners were angry and determined to fight harder.
- Southern slaves celebrated.
- Many slaves in the South did not even hear about the proclamation.
- Slavery continued in the South because the proclamation could not be enforced.

Lockbook of the Gettysburg Address

Materials: copies of pages 38 and 39, scissors, colored markers or pencils

In this activity, students create and illustrate a lockbook of the Gettysburg Address. You might want to encourage students to memorize the excerpt of the speech in the lockbook and recite it to the class. The illustrations that they create for each panel will help them visualize the text and aid in the memorization process. Before they recite, review with students the eight characteristics of good stage voice and presence, listed in the box on page 18.

CREATING THE LOCKBOOK

1. Copy the templates from pages 38 and 39 back to back so that panel 1 is behind the cover panel. Distribute a copy to each student.

2. Have students cut their pages horizontally along the dashed line to create two separate sheets with four panels each (two on the front and two on the back).

3. Ask students to fold the sheets in half vertically and then cut along the dotted lines. One sheet should have two slits, one at the top and one at the bottom. The other sheet should have a cut in the center of the folded edge (figure 1).

figure 1

4. Have students hold the sheet with the center slit so that panels 3 and 6 face them. Then have them curl panel 1 from the other sheet and feed it through the center hole between panels 3 and 6 (figure 2). Show them how to open up the page so it "locks" into place. Have students fold the lockbook pages and make sure that the pages are in proper order.

figure 2

5. On the cover, invite students to use creative lettering to title their books. Have them also create illustrations for each of the panels, depicting what Lincoln's words describe.

6. After students have completed their lockbooks, let them take turns reciting the speech excerpts to the class.

Eight Characteristics of Good Stage Voice and Presence

Rate: the speed at which one speaks
Projection: the volume at which one speaks
Clarity: the ability of the speaker to be understood
Expression: adding variety and feeling to one's speech
Pitch: the highs and lows of a person's speaking voice
Stance: standing straight and tall and confidently when speaking
Eye Contact: looking directly at the audience when speaking
Poise: the ability to recover quickly from a mistake and move on with confidence

Flip-Flop Autobiography of Black Soldiers

Materials: copies of page 40, white construction paper and glue sticks (optional), scissors, colored markers or pencils

African-American soldiers in the Civil War typically faced even more challenges than did white soldiers. Have your students research what life was like for the black soldiers who served in the Union army. Then have them create a flip-flop autobiography of an imaginary black soldier.

CREATING THE FLIP-FLOP BOOK

1. Provide students with copies of page 40. (They can glue this template to a sheet of white construction paper to give the project a more solid structure and a more finished look.)

2. Have students cut along each of the dotted lines on the template, making sure to stop where the dotted lines meet the solid line. Then have them fold down the flaps so that the writing lines are inside the fold.

3. Explain to students that they will be illustrating an aspect of the soldier's life on the cover flap and then writing about it on the lines inside. Remind students that this is an autobiography, so they should write in the first person.

4. On the first panel, have students write about the history of their soldier. Was he was a slave or a free man? What did he do before the war? The cover panel of this flap should depict the soldier before the war.

5. On the second panel, have students include information about why the soldier joined the army. What was going through his mind? What did he hope to accomplish? What role did he hope to play? On this cover flap, ask students to draw a picture of the soldier in uniform.

6. On the third panel, have students write about the discrimination the soldier faced, such as unequal pay, poorer quality food and clothing, having to perform menial duties, and so on. On the cover, have students illustrate an example of discrimination.

7. On the fourth panel, have students write about a battle in which their character fought. Where was it? What happened? Why did the battle take place? On the cover, have students draw a picture of the soldier in battle.

If you would like your students to create a more elaborate autobiography, have them tape two books together horizontally to create an eight-panel book. Hang the completed books on a bulletin board.

Comic Strip of Appomattox

Materials: copies of page 41, scissors, glue sticks, pencil, colored markers or pencils

Using the format of a comic strip, students explore the final days of the Civil War as seen through the eyes of Wilmer McLean, a farmer who had a unique perspective on these events. First, read aloud the story of Wilmer McLean in the box below, then have students complete the comic strip.

CREATING THE COMIC STRIP

1. Hand out copies of the comic strip template on page 41 and instruct students to cut along the dotted lines and glue the panels together into one long strip.

2. Have students first sketch their comic strip in pencil. Explain that their comic strip must include information about Bull Run, McLean's move to Appomattox, and the Confederate surrender, as well as a title. Each panel should include an illustration and dialogue, either written by hand or typed and glued into place.

3. After students have finalized their sketches, have them trace over the pencil with marker, write the comic strip title over the top of the first panel, and color in the drawing.

4. When students have finished drawing and coloring their comic strips, hang the projects on the bulletin board under a banner that reads "The Strange Case of Wilmer McLean."

The Strange Case of Wilmer McLean

Before the Civil War, Wilmer McLean lived the simple, quiet life of a farmer outside Manassas Junction, Virginia. After a shell exploded in his kitchen during the first major battle of the war, the Battle of Bull Run, Mr. McLean moved his family to safety nearly 200 miles away. He settled them in Appomattox Court House, Virginia. Nearly four years later, the Civil War came to an end. General Robert E. Lee agreed to meet with General Ulysses S. Grant to discuss the terms of the Confederate surrender. The generals were both near the town of Appomattox Court House and agreed to meet in the front parlor of a local farmer. Strange as it may seem, the parlor belonged to Wilmer McLean. After the meeting, Union officers stripped the room for souvenirs of this historic event. Later, Wilmer McLean was said to have boasted, "The war began in my front yard and ended in my front parlor."

Reconstruction Flapbook

Materials: copies of pages 42 and 43, scissors, stapler

The years after the Civil War brought many changes to the United States, especially to the South. In this activity, students create flapbooks that examine some of the issues of Reconstruction.

CREATING THE FLAPBOOK

1. Copy the templates on pages 42 and 43 back to back (panels 4, 5, and 6 on the back page should be upside down) and hand them out to students. Have students cut along the dotted lines to create three panels from each page (figure 1 below).

2. Have students place the panels on top of one another, overlapping them (figure 2).

3. Ask students to fold the tops of the panel backward—panels 4, 5, and 6 should show below panels 1, 2, and 3 (figure 3). The top can be fastened with two staples (figure 4).

4. Have students follow the directions to complete each of the panels on the flapbooks.

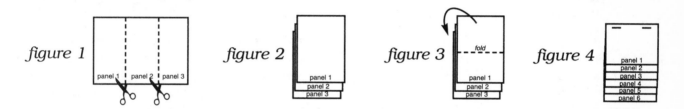

Suggested Answers for Flapbooks

Panel 2—Freedmen's Bureau:
provided food, clothing, medical supplies, fuel; gave out land; created schools; gave legal help

Panel 3—Presidential Reconstruction:
10% of voters in each southern state would have to swear loyalty to the United States; the state would have to ratify the 13th Amendment.

Panel 4—Congressional Reconstruction: the South would be governed by U.S. Army; blacks as well as whites would take part in creating a state's new constitution; Southerners who supported the Confederacy could not participate in the new government; blacks would be allowed to vote, hold office, and have same rights as whites.

Panel 5—Amendments:
The 13th Amendment outlawed slavery; the 14th Amendment made African-Americans citizens and gave them equal protection under the law; the 15th Amendment gave black men the right to vote.

Panel 6—Discrimination:
Paragraphs should include information about the Black Codes, which limited the rights of blacks. These laws forbade blacks from testifying against whites, bearing arms, and buying land in certain places. Blacks were segregated from whites in theaters, restaurants, hotels, streetcars, schools, parks, and other public places. Also, some white Southerners formed groups like the Ku Klux Klan that intimidated and even killed blacks.

Readers Theater: Ellen Craft: A Train Ride to Freedom

Materials: copies of pages 44–48

Reading plays aloud can provide students with opportunities to make connections between history and their own lives. Taking on a role, even for a short time, allows learners to become part of the story of our history, to become emotionally involved in the stories of other people, and to explore choices and lives foreign to their own.

Give each student a copy of the play *Ellen Craft: A Train Ride to Freedom* by Patricia Likens. Assign parts and have students read the play aloud. Consider having students perform the play for other classes or turn it into a radio play, complete with sound effects and music.

After the class reads the play, you may want to use the following activities to extend students' understanding of the Underground Railroad and the Civil War in general.

DIFFERENT DISGUISES

In order to gain freedom for herself and William, Ellen Craft had to disguise herself in men's clothes. In what other ways do students think that enslaved people had to disguise themselves? Encourage them to consider the situations of enslaved people who were denied an education but found ways to learn to read and write, who planned escapes on the Underground Railroad, and who tried to keep in touch with family members sent to other places.

HOME SWEET HOME

The Crafts' journey didn't end when they reached the North. To escape arrest under the Fugitive Slave Law, they had to flee to England. After their return from England, Ellen and William Craft eventually settled in Georgia. Ask your students if they find it surprising that Ellen and William moved their family back to the South instead of staying in the North. Ask students what factors might have prompted their decision.

THE UNDERGROUND RAILROAD

Many enslaved people in the South escaped to the North by means of the Underground Railroad. This well-traveled route had "conductors," such as Harriet Tubman, who guided their "passengers" to safety. Ask students to find out more about the workings of the Underground Railroad. To present their information, have them play the part of a free African-American newspaper reporter from the North who has assumed the disguise of an enslaved person escaping on the Underground Railroad. Ask them to write a series of newspaper articles describing their journey north.

Learning Poster of Civil Wars Today

Materials: poster board (about 3' by 4') in assorted colors, tape, glue sticks, colored markers or pencils, index cards, assorted craft materials, copier paper

A helpful way to bring the American Civil War into perspective with the present is to have students research civil wars that are currently being fought or that have occurred in the recent past. Have students work in groups of five or six to research and report on a civil war and create a learning poster. Below is a list of different elements students might include on their group poster.

CREATING THE LEARNING POSTER

Map of the Region: On a large sheet of white paper, have students draw a map of the region where the civil war is occurring. Maps should include major cities, important battle sites, and significant landforms.

Government: On an index card (or two), have students write a description of the area's government: its political system and structure, its leaders, its opposition, and so on.

History: Have students write a brief history of the origins of the civil war. You may want to have them present this as a lockbook (see page 17) or simply write the information on an index card. Encourage them to include photos from newsmagazines if possible or draw pictures.

Time Line: Have students create a time line of the civil war, beginning with the earliest events and continuing up to the most recent ones.

Reasons for Conflict: Invite students to create a graphic organizer (such as a web) that lists some of the reasons why the two (or more) factions are at war. They might also create a multicolumn chart that compares the different factions' reasons for fighting.

Point of View Letters: Have students write letters from the points of view of two soldiers fighting on different sides of the civil war. The letters should be written in the first person and detail the reasons why the soldier is willing to sacrifice his or her life for the cause.

Famous People: Have students create a portrait and brief biography of two famous people who have been involved in the civil war. Give them the option of creating a people book (see page 13) for each of these individuals.

Peace Treaty: As a group, have students discuss ways that the conflict might be resolved. Then have them design and write a peace treaty that they think would be fair to both sides and bring an end to the war.

As students finish each element, have them add it in an organized way to their group's poster board. Each group should use a different colored sheet. Display the completed posters under a banner titled "Civil Wars in the World Today."

Civil War Study Guide

Create a wonderful study guide for students by having them compile all of their mini-books, activities, and projects into an interactive Civil War "textbook." Over the course of the unit, ask students to save all of their papers and projects in a pocket folder. At the end of the unit, use a binding machine to put them all together. If you don't have access to one, use a three-hole punch and yarn. Here are suggestions for compiling each page.

Materials: all of the projects students have created, glue sticks, 8½" by 11" paper, binding machine (if available) or hole punch with yarn

COVER

When binding the study guides, add a page of heavy stock to the front and back. Have students use creative lettering to add a title to the cover and then draw a total of ten icons around the front and back covers. The icons can represent any ten things students learned over the course of the unit. Ask them to number the icons and then, on the inside front cover, write a complete sentence describing the significance of each.

PAGE 1

Have students glue the top edge of their FREEDOM QUILT to the first page. This allows the quilt square to be lifted so the writing can be seen. Be sure students include a title for the page.

Nathan's Freedom Quilt
Lift the quilt block to find the secret to freedom!

Warren's ROAD MAP to the Civil War

PAGE 2

Students can glue the back panel of the folded ROAD MAP TO THE CIVIL WAR to this page. The map can then be opened easily while still remaining attached to the interactive textbook.

PAGE 3

Have students glue the flap of their LETTER TO THE PRESIDENT to this page. The envelope can then be lifted, allowing the letter to be pulled out.

Dear Mr. President

ABRAHAM LINCOLN
THE WHITE HOUSE
WASHINGTON, DC

BEAU TARLTON
TARA PLANTATION
ATLANTA, GA

PAGE 4

ABE LINCOLN'S RÉSUMÉ can simply be bound in as page 4.

Abraham Lincoln
1600 Pennsylvania Avenue • Washington, DC
abelincoln@hotmail.com

EDUCATION

Early Education
Attended school sporadically from 1815 due to plowing and planting.
Borrowed books and read whenever possible.
In 1831 I settled in New Salem, Illinois where I learned basic math, read Shakespeare, participates in local debating society.

Law School
Received law license - September 9, 1836

POLITICAL
EXPERIENCE

First Political Speech • 1830
• Spoke in favor of improving navigation on the Sangamon River

Candidate for Illinois General Assembly • 1832
• Lost my first election : (

Appointed Postmaster of New Salem and Deputy County Surveyor • 1833

Elected to the Illinois General Assembly • 1834
• Assemblyman as a member of the Whig party

Re-elected to the Illinois General Assembly • 1836
• Now a leader of the Whig party

Re-elected to the Illinois General Assembly • 1838
• Whig floor leader

Re-elected to the Illinois General Assembly • 1840

Campaigned for Henry Clay in the Presidential Election • 1844

Elected to the U.S. House of Representatives • 1846

Campaigned for Zachary Taylor in Massachusetts and Illinois • 1848

Re-enters Politics Opposing the Kansas-Nebraska Act • 1854
• Elected to Illinois legislature but declined in order to try to become U.S. Senator (don't get chosen)

Helped Organize the Republican Party of Illinois • 1856
• Received 110 votes at Republican Convention for vice-presidential nomination; campaigned in Illinois for Republican presidential candidate, John C. Frémont

Spoke Out Against the Dred Scott Decision • 1857

Nominated to be Republican Senator from Illinois • 1858
• Stephen Douglas and I engage in seven debates; he is chosen over me.

PAGE 5

Students can collapse their CLINCHER and create a pocket on this page to hold the flattened manipulative. They can create the pocket by folding a piece of 8½" by 11" paper in half horizontally, slipping another sheet of paper into the fold, and taping the edges. Encourage students to add a title and to decorate the page.

5 6
8 2
3

Advantages of the North and South

PAGE 6

Instruct students to glue the back of their MATCHBOOK OF A NATION DIVIDED onto this page. They can add a decorative border.

Union and Confederate States

A Nation Divided

PAGE 7

Students can create a pocket-page like they did for page 5 to hold their JUMPING JACK. You might have them write a paragraph on the front of the pocket that describes the accomplishment of this famous historical figure.

ABRAHAM LINCOLN JUMPING JACK

My People Book of Harriet Tubman

PAGE 8

Have students glue the back of their PEOPLE BOOK to this page. The arms can then be folded across the figure's chest, allowing the interactive textbook to close.

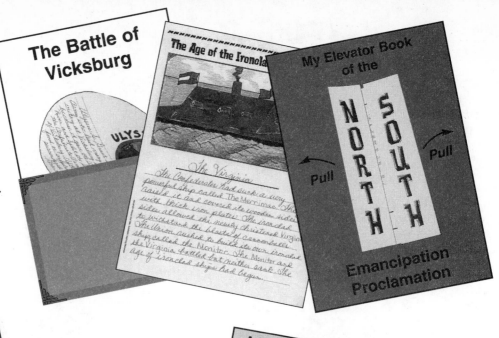

PAGE 9

Students can create a pocket-page to hold their CIRCLE BOOK OF FAMOUS BATTLES.

PAGE 10

THE AGE OF IRONCLAD SHIPS activity sheet can be bound in as page 10.

PAGE 11

Have students glue the back of the ELEVATOR BOOK to page 11.

PAGE 12

Ask students to create a pocket-page to hold their LOCKBOOK OF THE GETTYSBURG ADDRESS. Have them decorate the front pocket with either a picture or a paragraph related to this historic event.

PAGE 13

Ask students to turn their FLIP-FLOP AUTOBIOGRAPHY sideways and glue it onto this page.

PAGE 14

Instruct students to fold the COMIC STRIP OF APPOMATTOX in half and glue it to page 14. The strip can then be opened to reveal all of the panels.

PAGE 15

Finally, have students glue the back of their FLAPBOOK OF THE RECONSTRUCTION to this page.

Civil War Vocabulary

word: _____

definition: _____
_____
_____

word: _____

definition: _____
_____
_____

Freedom Quilt Template

Use geometric shapes to illustrate a hidden message for a fugitive slave, instructing him or her how to find a safe path to freedom. Color the shapes so that they look like pieces of fabric and then cut out the quilt block. On the back of the quilt, write a paragraph describing the message conveyed by your quilt.

Clincher of North and South

1. Fold the top right corner of the paper down diagonally to the left so that the top edge aligns with the left edge. Crease along the fold.

2. Cut off the bottom strip so that you are left with an 8½" inch square.

3. Fold the top left corner down diagonally so that the top edge of the paper aligns with the right edge, and then crease the fold. You should now have an X-shaped fold in the paper when it is open.

4. Fold all four corners so that they meet at the center point.

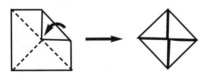

5. Turn this square over (while it's still folded) and again fold all four corners in so that they meet at the center point.

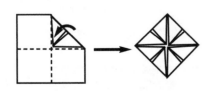

6. Put the shape flat on your desk. On each of the 8 triangular sections, randomly write a different number from 1 to 8.

7. Place your index finger at the center point where the four corners meet. With your other hand, lift one of the four corners and pull the flap on the underside outward so it opens into a conelike shape. Open all four corners this way.

8. Put your index fingers and thumbs into the cones and make the points of the cones meet. You can now move your fingers back and forth so that the clincher opens horizontally and vertically.

9. Follow your teacher's directions for creating a Civil War quiz with the clincher.

Matchbook of a Nation Divided

Copy the questions below on the back of the map template on page 31 so that they appear inverted, as shown below.

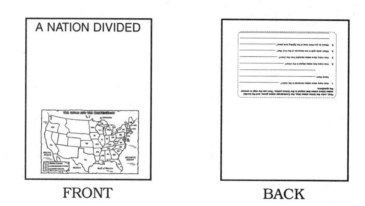

FRONT   BACK

First, color the Union states blue, the Confederate states green, and the border states (slave states that stayed in the Union) yellow. Then use the map to answer the questions.

1. How many slave states remained in the Union? _____

    Name them: _____

    _____

2. How many free states stayed in the Union? _____

3. How many slave states seceded from the Union? _____

4. Which state split in two because of the Civil War? _____

5. Where do you think most of the fighting took place? _____

    _____

A Nation Divided

Hands-On History: Civil War, Scholastic Teaching Resources, page 31

Jumping Jacks of Famous Men

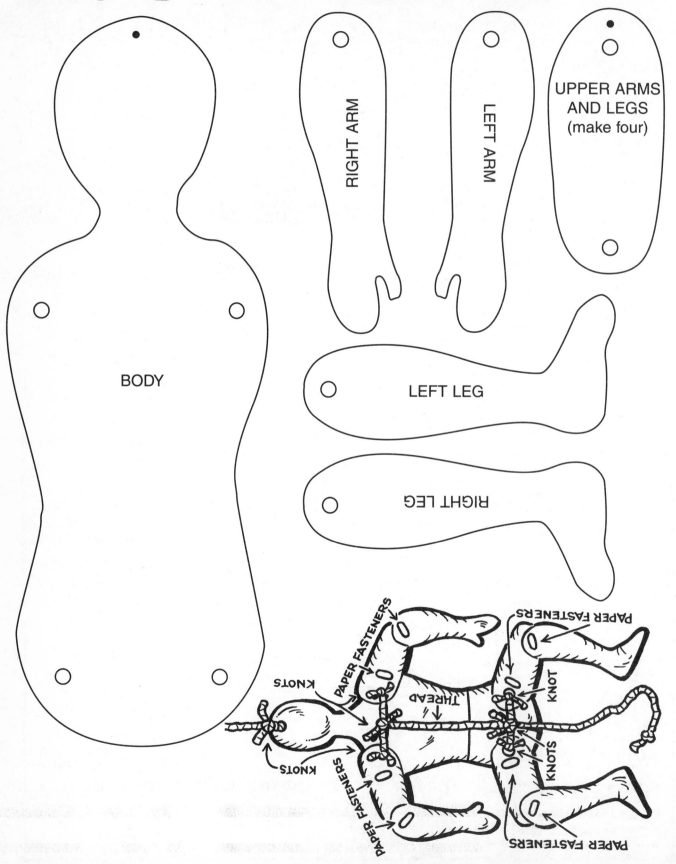

RIGHT ARM

LEFT ARM

UPPER ARMS
AND LEGS
(make four)

BODY

LEFT LEG

RIGHT LEG

PAPER FASTENERS

PAPER FASTENERS

PAPER FASTENERS

KNOTS

KNOTS

THREAD

KNOT

KNOTS

PAPER FASTENERS

PAPER FASTENERS

Circle Book Drawing Template

Page 1: Fill in the circle with the name and date of the battle you've chosen and include a drawing or map to illustrate it. Then fold the page along the dotted line. Reopen the page and cut out the circle.

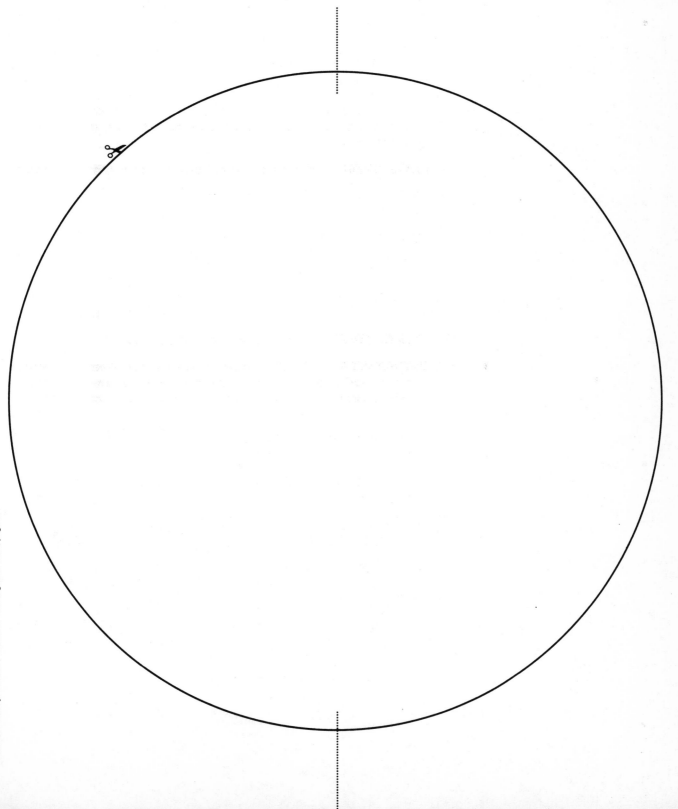

Circle Book Writing Template

Page 2: Write a brief account of the battle, describing who was involved, why and where it took place, and what the results were. Then fold the page along the dotted line. Reopen the page and cut out the circle.

Circle Book Drawing/Writing Template

Page 3: Report on a famous person who took part in the battle. Draw a picture of the person at the top and write a description in the bottom half.

Page 4: Design a monument for the battlefield. Draw a picture of the monument at the top and write a paragraph explaining the monument's design in the bottom half. Then fold the page along the dotted line. Reopen the page and cut out the circle.

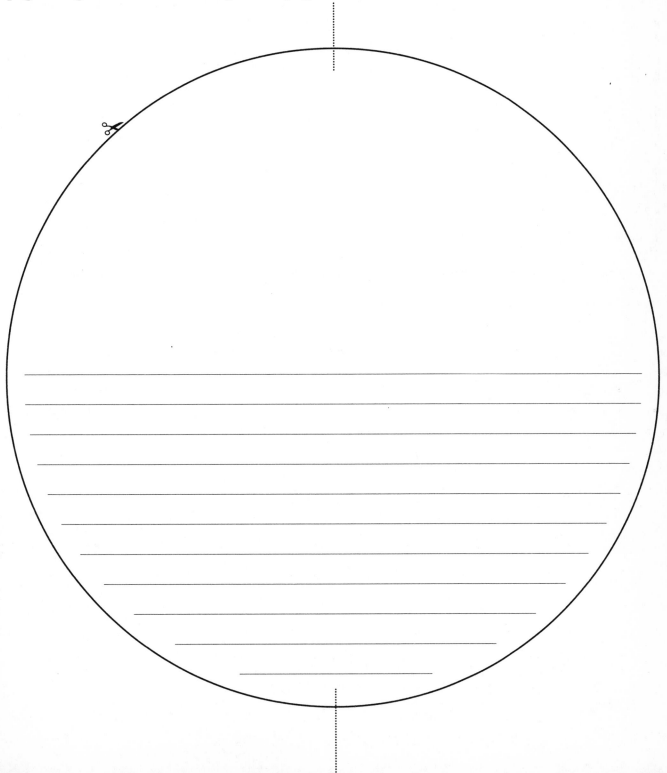

The Age of Ironclad Ships

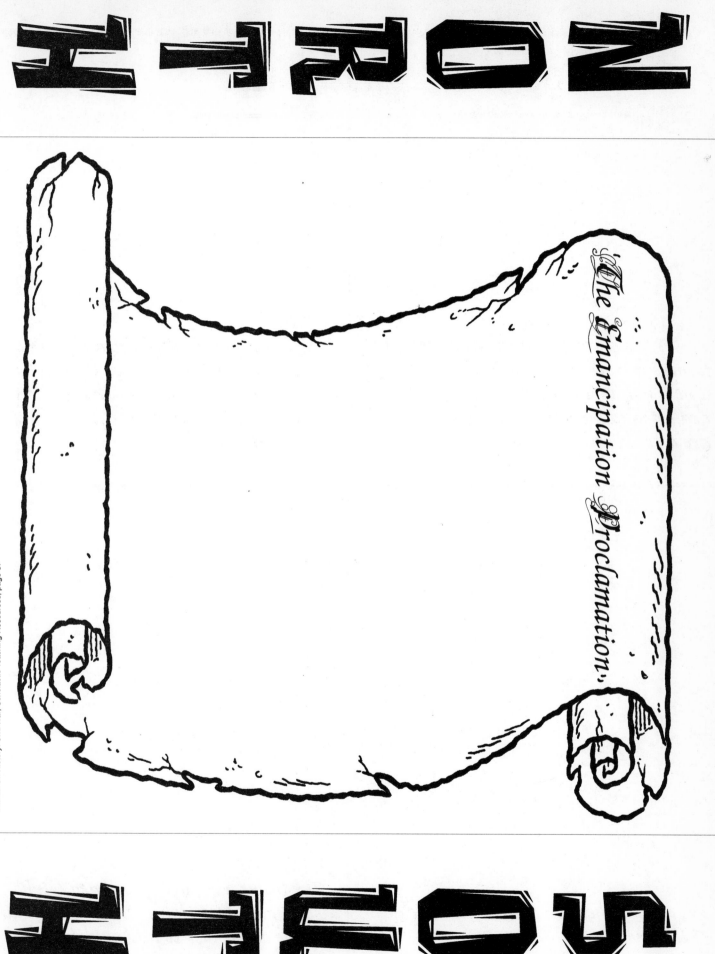

The Emancipation Proclamation.

Hands-On History: Civil War, Scholastic Teaching Resources, page 37

Four score and seven years ago our fathers brought forth, upon this continent, a new nation, conceived in Liberty, and dedicated to the proposition that all men are created equal.

1

We have come to dedicate a portion of it, as a final resting place for those who here gave their lives that that nation might live. It is altogether fitting and proper that we should do this.

4

We are met here on a great battlefield of that war.

3

The brave men, living and dead, who struggled, here, have consecrated it far above our power to add or detract.

6

But in a larger sense, we can not dedicate—we can not consecrate—we can not hallow—this ground.

5

Hands-On History: Civil War, Scholastic Teaching Resources, page 39

The world will little note, nor long remember, what we say here, but can never forget what they did here.

7

Now we are engaged in a great civil war, testing whether that nation, or any nation, so conceived, and so dedicated, can long endure.

2

Comic Strip Template

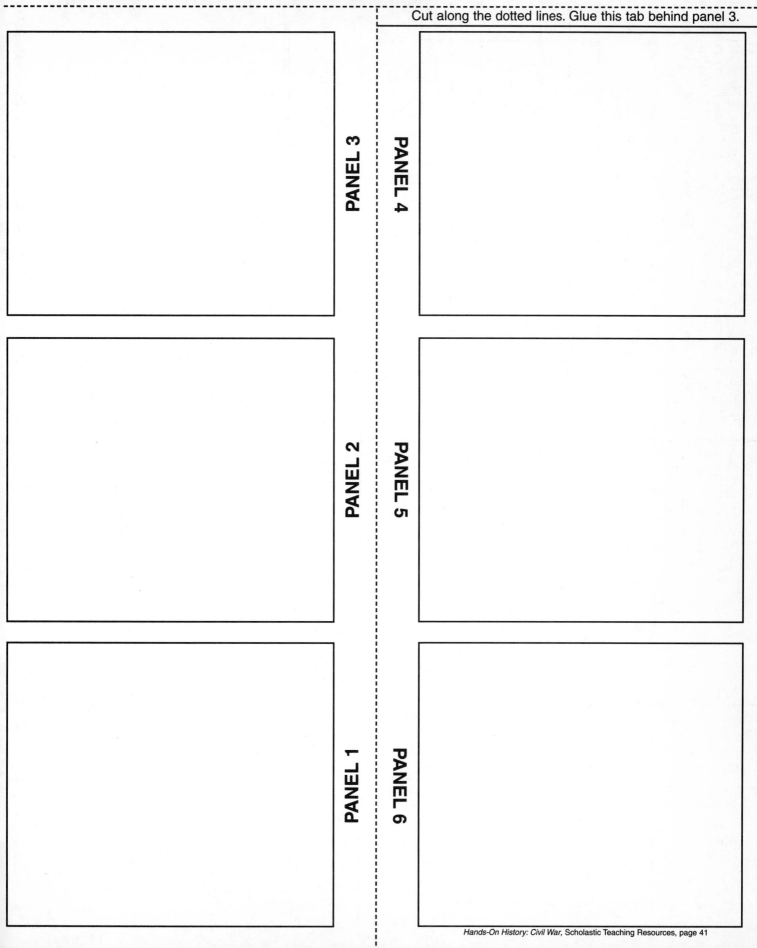

Cut along the dotted lines. Glue this tab behind panel 3.

PANEL 3

PANEL 4

PANEL 2

PANEL 5

PANEL 1

PANEL 6

During the time of Reconstruction, the 13th, 14th, and 15th Amendments were passed. On the lines below, describe the meaning of each amendment.

Presidential Reconstruction

Write a paragraph describing the discrimination that African Americans faced in the years after the Civil War. Be sure to include information about the Black Codes, segregation, and the Ku Klux Klan.

3. Presidential Reconstruction

2. The Freedmen's Bureau

1. Title and Name

Create a thought web by drawing lines from the center oval to facts that describe Congress's ideas for Reconstruction.

Congressional Reconstruction

4. Congressional Reconstruction

Create a thought web by drawing lines from the center oval to facts that describe President Lincoln's plans for Reconstruction.

5. The Amendments

Write a list of ways in which the Freedmen's Bureau helped both blacks and whites in the South after the Civil War.

6. Discrimination

Ellen Craft: A Train Ride to Freedom

by Patricia Likens

Cast of Characters

(in order of appearance)

Narrator
William Craft: Enslaved man and Ellen's husband
Ellen Craft: Enslaved woman
Ticket Agent
Train Conductor 1
William Cray: A white passenger
Captain Sherman: A steamship captain
Mr. Pruett: A slave dealer
Custom Officer
Percy Jackson: A white passenger
Yankee Soldier
Train Conductor 2

Act 1

Scene 1: November 1848. Macon, Georgia.

NARRATOR: Ellen Craft was the daughter of a white man and an African-American enslaved woman. Ellen, too, was considered a slave. At the age of 11, she was sent to work at a house in Macon, Georgia. There Ellen met William Craft, an enslaved man who worked in the same house until he was hired out as a cabinetmaker. Several years later, Ellen and William received permission from their owners to marry. Soon, they were planning their escape from slavery.

WILLIAM CRAFT: If I didn't know it was you, I wouldn't know it was you.

ELLEN CRAFT (*doubtfully*): We must be crazy. Who's going to believe that I'm an old white man? Just because I'm wearing men's clothes and my skin is light doesn't mean I'm going to fool anybody. What about my voice? My voice is sure to give me away.

WILLIAM CRAFT: You're Mr. Johnson—a sick, old white man. Just groan a lot and shake your head. Besides, I'll be right there to answer any questions.

ELLEN CRAFT (*groaning and shaking her head*): How's that?

WILLIAM CRAFT: Not bad, not bad. One thing we've got to figure out is what to do when somebody asks you to read or write.

ELLEN CRAFT: I'm pretending to be old and sick, right? What if we put my arm in a sling? You can explain that I can't write because I've hurt my arm. I can pretend that my eyes are bad, too.

WILLIAM CRAFT: That ought to take care of it. Now, all we need to do is get permission to leave Macon for a few days at Christmas. Once we do that, I'll buy our tickets. (*whistling*) Macon, Georgia, to Philadelphia, Pennsylvania. I've never traveled so far in my life.

ELLEN CRAFT: It's a long trip from slavery to freedom. I expect it's the longest trip we'll ever take.

Scene 2: December 21, 1848. Early morning at the Macon, Georgia, train station.

NARRATOR: Ellen and William were given permission to leave Macon over Christmas. Their escape was underway! Ellen bundled herself in men's clothes that she'd sewn herself. She wrapped a muffler around her face and put her arm in a sling. Ellen Craft, an enslaved African-American woman, was now Mr. Johnson, a free white man. At the train station, William walked a few steps behind his "master," Mr. Johnson.

ELLEN CRAFT: Two tickets to Savannah, please, for myself and my servant.

TICKET AGENT: Two tickets to Savannah, coming right up! Here you go, sir. You'll be in the first car. Your man will be in the last car with the other blacks.

ELLEN CRAFT: No! You can see that I'm injured, I've hurt my arm. I need to have my servant in the same car with me.

TICKET AGENT: Sorry, sir, but you know the rules as well as I do. No slaves in the first cars. You need anything, one of the conductors or porters will be more than happy to help you.

TRAIN CONDUCTOR 1: ALL ABOARD!

WILLIAM CRAFT: That's all right, Mr. Johnson. The conductor, he'll take good care of you. You'll be fine. I'll find you when we get to the Savannah station. You just wait for me to find you, 'cause I will now.

NARRATOR: Ellen boards the first car reluctantly, watching as William goes to the last car. She sits in a seat beside the window and stares out of it. Suddenly, Ellen recognizes a familiar face.

ELLEN CRAFT (*to herself*): Mr. Cray! It can't be! Oh, please, don't let him get on this train.

(*William Cray walks into the car and stops beside Ellen's seat.*)

WILLIAM CRAY: Excuse me, sir. Is this seat taken?

(*Ellen shakes her head and turns her face to the window again.*)

WILLIAM CRAY: Fine morning, isn't it? (*He pauses.*) I said (*in a louder voice*), it's a fine morning, isn't it?

(*Ellen coughs.*)

WILLIAM CRAY: You're not sick, are you, sir? I can't afford to catch anything at Christmastime. Maybe I'll just move a few rows down. You don't mind, do you? Can't take any chances. (*He hurries to another seat.*)

ELLEN CRAFT (*softly to herself*): No, sir, can't afford to take any chances.

Act 2

Scene 1: The next day. Aboard a steamer bound for Charleston, South Carolina.

NARRATOR: Ellen and William were reunited at the Savannah train station. They spent the night at a hotel in the city: Ellen stayed in a room, while William slept in the quarters set aside for enslaved people traveling with their owners. The next morning, they boarded a steamer headed for Charleston, South Carolina, and were separated again. At dinner, Ellen found herself at a table with the steamer captain and a slave dealer.

CAPTAIN SHERMAN: Your boy seems to be very helpful to you, Mr. Johnson.

ELLEN CRAFT: He is, Captain. I treat William well, and he respects that.

MR. PRUETT: You treat him well? Whatever for? He's a slave. He doesn't need respect. All he needs is a little food and water, some clothes on his back, and a short leash. You're a fool to travel north with him. He'll leave you lickety-split once you hit Philadelphia—see if he don't.

ELLEN CRAFT: I trust William. I would never mistreat him. That's why I know he would never leave me. He doesn't have to go north to live a better life.

MR. PRUETT: Tell you what, I'll give you my card. When he runs off on you, you get in touch with me. I'll find him. I'll sell him for you, too, if that's what you want. I could get a good piece of change for him at auction.

ELLEN CRAFT: No matter what happens, William is not for sale. He never will be. He'll never be separated from his family. Never.

CAPTAIN SHERMAN: Ah, Mr. Johnson, I'm sorry to say that Mr. Pruett's probably right. Once your William sets foot on Northern soil, I'm afraid he'll run away. I've seen it happen too many times. It doesn't matter how well or how badly you treat your slaves. They'll run away every time.

ELLEN CRAFT (*calming down*): Then I'll be sure to keep my eyes on William, Captain.

Act 3

Scene 1: Christmas Eve, 1848. At the Baltimore, Maryland, train station.

NARRATOR: The Crafts arrived in Charleston, South Carolina, and then journeyed to Baltimore, Maryland, the last Southern city on their trip. The next stop would be the Northern city of Philadelphia. There they would be free. But a Maryland law almost derailed Ellen and William.

CUSTOM OFFICER: Look, if you insist on taking a slave north with you, Mr. Johnson, you have to sign and post a bond. It's the law in Maryland. How do I know you're not some white abolitionist, pretending to own this slave here? How do I know you won't set him free the minute you get to Philadelphia?

ELLEN CRAFT: I understand all that, but you can see, sir, that I've injured my hand. I can't use it at all. How can you expect me to sign anything?

CUSTOM OFFICER: How do I know you're not pretending to have a hurt hand? Sign with your other hand, then. Do that, post your one dollar fee, and you're free to go.

ELLEN CRAFT: I have arthritis in my other hand. I can't possibly write with it.

CUSTOM OFFICER: I guess your slave will be staying right here in Baltimore, then. Enjoy your trip, Mr. Johnson.

WILLIAM CRAFT: Pardon me, sir, but Mr. Johnson really can't sign the bond. He hasn't been able to use his hands for a month now. That's why I'm traveling with him. He can give you the dollar—

CUSTOM OFFICER: What's the matter? Don't you want to stay here in Baltimore?

NARRATOR: Just then, Percy Jackson, a passenger on the same train that Ellen (disguised as Mr. Johnson) and William took from Charleston to Baltimore, walks past. He overhears the argument and walks over.

PERCY JACKSON: Mr. Johnson? What's the trouble here?

ELLEN CRAFT: This officer says I must sign a bond so William can go north with me, but I can't sign anything because of my hands.

PERCY JACKSON: Officer, what if I sign for Mr. Johnson? I can vouch for him; we traveled in together on the train from Charleston. He's a decent Southern gentleman, not an abolitionist. He's only bringing William along because he needs medical care. Will that do?

CUSTOM OFFICER: It's your name, sir. I guess you can sign it to anything you want to.

ELLEN CRAFT: Thank you, Mr. Jackson. You don't know what this means to me.

WILLIAM CRAFT: Merry Christmas, Mr. Jackson!

Scene 2: Christmas Eve, 1848. Aboard a train about to leave Baltimore for Philadelphia.

NARRATOR: Thanks to Mr. Jackson, Ellen and William were able to board the train for Philadelphia. For the last time, William helped "Mr. Johnson" get settled in the "whites only" car and returned to the car where blacks had to sit. On the way, William ran into a Yankee soldier.

YANKEE SOLDIER: Hold it! What are you doing in this car? It's for whites only.

WILLIAM CRAFT: I was helping Mr. Johnson. He's my master. He's been very sick.

(*Ellen hears William's voice outside her window. She pulls back the curtains and listens.*)

YANKEE SOLDIER: So you say. Get your master. I want to see for myself how sick he's been.

WILLIAM CRAFT: He's not going to like being disturbed. I just got him all settled—

YANKEE SOLDIER: Just get him. I want to see you two in the train station office in five minutes.

ELLEN CRAFT (*opening the window*): What's all the commotion? How's a sick man supposed to get any rest with all this racket going on? William! What are you doing? Get on this train! What if it leaves without you? What will I do then? Who'll take care of me? Stop dawdling and get aboard. (*looking at the Yankee soldier*) Who are you? Why are you outside my window yelling?

WILLIAM CRAFT: That's Mr. Johnson, officer. Mr. Johnson, my master.

YANKEE OFFICER: Sorry, sir, but I can't let you through to Philadelphia unless you show me a document that says you're ill—

ELLEN CRAFT: Document! Haven't I already paid and signed a bond? Can't you Yankees see? Don't I look like a sick man? What do you need a piece of paper for?

TRAIN CONDUCTOR 2 (*hurrying up to the train*): Mr. Johnson! What's the matter? Do you need a doctor? Are you feeling worse?

YANKEE SOLDIER: Do you know this man?

TRAIN CONDUCTOR 2: He came into Baltimore on my train. Mr. Johnson's been pretty sick, but William takes good care of him. Oh! You don't think William's going to jump off this train and run away? He wouldn't leave Mr. Johnson. Would you, William?

WILLIAM CRAFT (*smiling*): No, sir. Nothing could make me leave Mr. Johnson.

ELLEN CRAFT: Thank you, conductor. I'm going to write a letter to the railroad telling them how helpful you've been. (*to the officer*) Are we free to leave now?

YANKEE SOLDIER: Yes, sir. Sorry about the trouble.

ELLEN CRAFT: No harm done. Would you just make sure that William gets on the train without any more trouble? Thank you, officer.

NARRATOR: Ellen and William Craft arrived safely in Philadelphia on Christmas Day, 1848. Ellen resumed her real identity, and they both took their place in society as free people.